To Dad with love

Xma

— In the hope th
you'll be able
and see for yourself...

山川草木

前田真三写真集

前田真三写真集 山川草木

THIS LAND··· THIS BEAUTY

Japan's Natural Splendor

CALLIGRAPHY : RYU HORIUCHI
DESIGN & LAYOUT : GO ASANUMA+G&A STUDIO
TRANSLATION : ERNEST & MATSUE RICHTER

日本の自然

前田真三

我が国は北緯25度から45度にかけて、アジア大陸の東のはずれに弓状の列島をつくっている。周囲を海に囲まれた島国であり、地形が複雑で、気象条件も極めて変化に富んでいる。気候区分では温帯に属し、海洋性の気候を示している。降水量は多く、湿度も高い。また上空には強い西風のジェット気流が流れているため、おおむね西から天気が変わりやすく、気象の変化も激しい。夏はむし暑く、冬は寒く、春と秋には天気が変わりやすいというのも大きな特徴であろう。

以上の事柄が日本の自然に大きな影響を与えていることは当然であるが、我々日本人の生活にも深いかかわりを持っていることもまた明白である。例えば、良い意味では季節の変化に微妙に対応する繊細な神経もここから生まれてきたものであろうし、反面こせこせと何時も追いかけられているような国民性もこういった気象条件から生まれたものであると思われる。

複雑で変化に富んだ地形を持つ我が国の国土は、その70パーセント以上が緑に履われており、四季の変化が表わす自然の美しさは世界の中でも非常に勝れていると言われる。その豊かな自然に恵まれすぎているため、日本人はかえって木を切ることも鳥獣を捕えることにも余り疑問を持つことな

く生活してきたという一面がある。しかし昨今のように機械力によって広い地域の開発が急速に進むと、自然の回復力をはるかに上回る破壊が進んで、これを防止しようという反省の動きが起こり、自然保護の必要性が叫ばれるようになった。本来自然界は、動物、植物を含めて長い間お互いに競争し合ったり、助けあったりする中でバランスが保たれてきた。人間も自然の一員としてこのバランスの担い手であったわけであるが、文明が進むにつれてこのバランスが崩れ、益々その傾向が強くなりつつあるのが我が国の実状である。

如何に文明が進んでも所詮人間も動物であるから、長い間自然から離れて生活していると、美しい自然や静かな自然を求める欲求が顕著になるのは当然である。人は本質的に自然を慈しみ、自然に憧れる心を持っている。現在のように都市化が進めば進む程、自然の中に安らぎと憩いを求める心は更に強くなる筈である。我々日本人は、昔から自然を愛し、自然とともに心豊かに生きてきた。経済だけの繁栄はあり得ない筈で、国際社会の一員としての責任を果たすことも勿論大切であるが、この豊かな自然を子々孫々に伝えるための努力こそ現代の日本人に課せられた最も大きな義務ではないだろうか。

JAPAN AND NATURE

Shinzo Maeda

The Japanese archipelago lies off the eastern end of the Asian continent and is a bow-shaped strand of islands stretching from 25 to 45 degrees north latitude. An island nation, Japan is a land of varied geographical features and atmospheric phenomena, and its temperate-oceanic climate is greatly influenced by the strong jet stream which moves over it from the west. The weather is quite changeable in the spring and fall, but the most distinctive features of the climate are the rainy, humid summers and the cold, dry winter months. These environmental factors have clearly influenced the nature and lifestyle of the Japanese, helping to make them a hard-working people, and at the same time nurturing a sensitivity and ability to adapt to the changing seasons.

More than 70 percent of our country's varied geography is covered with greenery and it can be said that the natural beauty of her four seasons vies with that of any place in the world. Unfortunately, however, the richness of our natural environment has led us to prodigality in the use of our resources, and we have come to live without due regard for the preservation of our land and its flora and fauna. Powerful machines move over the land, leveling and developing——destroying with a speed that outstrips nature's recuperative powers. Man, who is but one part of the natural order, is now asserting himself with a speed and impact that is throwing our natural environment badly out of balance. And in Japan, as in other places, the situation is worsening. But today some people are finally beginning to move against development, to call for deeper consideration of our role in the environment and the need to protect nature. They remind us that man can never escape the fact that he, too, is an animal, a part of the environment. As such it is only natural that, despite his recent extrangement from nature, he carries within him a desire for its beauty and serenity. In our hearts we love nature—— revere it——and so it is that even as we develope our country, we find that the more we develope, the more we crave the peace of mind and relaxation that can only be found in the very things we are pushing aside.

Man has long lived in harmony with nature; he cannot live in a world solely devoted to economic prosperity. To be sure, Japan must meet her responsibilities as an industrial power in the society of nations, but we must exert every effort to preserve and hand down to our descendants the treasures of nature with which we have been blessed. That is our greatest—— our most solemn duty.

私の生家は、高くはないが三方を山に囲まれた山村にある。耕地面積は少なく、ほとんどが杉、桧や雑木の山で、野鳥の種類なども多く、家の周囲にはあり余る程の豊かな自然があった。

小学校から旧制中学に進む頃にかけて、私は野鳥に夢中になっていった。ひまさえあれば野鳥を追って、村内で一番高い陣馬山から八王子城跡の城山など、付近の山を我家の庭のように走り回ったものである。旧制中学に進んで、友人等と山岳部をつくり、八ヶ岳や北アルプス方面にも出掛けるようになった。

戦後社会人となっても山歩きを続けていたが、何時の頃からかカメラを持って山を歩くようになった。そして様々な山と出会い、またその山で様々な人と出会った。そのことが後に写真の道に入るきっかけともなった。

I was born in a mountain village in a house surrounded by wooded hills. Not much of the area was cultivated; most of it was groves of cedars, Japanese cypress and mixed timber. Nature was everywhere around my home, and when I was in the sixth and seventh grades, I was very interested in wild birds. Whenever I could, I ran after the birds around Mt. Jimba and the nearby ruins of Hachioji Castle. Those hills were like my own back yard.

When I was in high school, my friends and I organized a mountaineering club, and we climbed the Yatsugatake Mountains or the higher peaks in the Northern Japan Alps. I continued my mountain climbing even after I became an office worker following World War II, and it was sometime during those days that I started to take my camera with me on my trips to the mountains. There I encountered the scenery and the people that later led to my becoming a photographer.

私の生家の前には多摩川の支流である北浅川が流れている。小学生の頃から夏休みなどは、宿題そっちのけにして終日川遊びで明け暮れたものである。

大きな川ではないが、当時はヤマメ、ハヤ、ナマズ、ウナギ等がたくさん棲んでいた。特にウナギやナマズを獲る為に前の晩から流し針を仕掛けておき、翌朝暗いうちに起きて、これをたぐってゆく時の緊張感は、現在のいい風景に出会った時の緊張感と似ているような気がする。

後年写真の道に入り何となく水の写真を多く撮るようになり、また私自身渓流や渓谷を写すことに強くひかれていったのも、少年の頃のそうした思いが心の片隅に残っていたからかもしれない。

The Kita Asakawa River, a branch of the Tama River, runs in front of the house where I was born. As a schoolboy, I used to spend all day on that river, especially during the summer vacations. I might add that as a consequence I never touched my homework.

The Kita Asakawa is not a large river, but in those days it held plenty of trout, dace, catfish and eels. We would set drift hooks at night for the catfish and eels, and the next morning we would get up before dawn and check our lines. That was long ago, but for some reason, the feeling of excitement I once had when pulling in those lines now returns to me whenever I come upon beautiful scenery.

Since growing up and becoming a photographer, I have somehow had a tendency to take pictures of water, and I have become increasingly interested in photographs of mountain streams and gorges. That may well be the result of my boyhood experiences, for in a corner of my heart there is nostalgia for the stream of my youth.

私の父は絵や書を描き、俳句などもよくする風流人であったので、家のしきたりに従って様々な年中行事を丹念に行なっていた。

節分の時に使う柊や仲秋の名月に使うオミナエシなどを山から採ってくるのは、何時も私の仕事であった。当時野鳥を追って山野を駆けめぐり、何処の山に行けば何があるかを私が一番良く知っていたからである。そのころでもオミナエシが群落で咲いているところを知っていたのは私一人であった。そこは川村官林と称する御料林(国有林)の中の僅かに開けた一角であった。その付近は、当時昼なお暗い樅や桧の原生林であった。

その山も今では明るい霊園と化して、全く昔日の面影はない。生家に帰る道すがら時折そこを通るが、そのたびにオミナエシのことが頭をかすめる。

My father was a man of refined tastes, one who enjoyed such things as painting, poetry and calligraphy. He was a man who never missed any family events or traditional functions, and he led the family in celebrating them. It was always my duty to go to the hillside to gather holly branches for the celebration of *setsubun*, on the day before the beginning of spring, or to pick the yellow flowers used in the harvest moon festival. This was because my youthful romps around the hills and fields in pursuit of wild birds had thoroughly acquainted me with our area, and I was the one who best knew where to go for whatever we needed. Only I knew where those yellow flowers bloomed in abundance; they grew in one small corner of an open space in the Imperial Forest called Kawamura Kanrin. That area was a virgin forest of firs and Japanese cypress, a dark place even in the daytime. The place has since become a bright cemetery park, and there is no longer even the slightest trace of the old days. But now when I sometimes pass by there on the way to my parents' home, I am always reminded of the yellow flowers of fall.

私の生家は山林業を営んでいたから、木との
かかわりあいは生まれると同時に始まったと
いっていいかも知れない。
小学生の頃から休日には山仕事に入る人達と
一緒によく山に行った。木樵が切り倒した木
にムササビの巣があってその子を持ち帰って
育てたり、リスの子をつかまえたことなども
あった。
旧制中学三年の頃だったと思うが、裏の竹藪
の中にかなり大きな榎の木があった。私が何
の目的でその木を切ったか失念したが、その
時父はものすごい形相で怒った。そして言っ
た、「我家は山林によって生計を立てている。
植えた木は勿論、自然に生えた木でもむやみ
に切ってはならない。」その言葉は、今でも肝
に銘じている。

My father made his living in the forestry busi-
ness and, therefore, I might say that I was born
into a close relationship with trees. As a young
schoolboy, I used to go to the mountains with
my father's employees when there was no
school. Once we happened to find the nest of a
flying squirrel on a tree that had been felled by
a lumberjack, and we took those baby flying
squirrels home and raised them. On another
occasion, I myself, caught a baby squirrel.
There was a big hackberry tree in the bamboo
grove behind our house, and one day——I think
I was in ninth grade at the time——I cut down
that tree for some reason or other. When my
father found out, he was furious. "Our family,"
he said, "makes a living from the forests, and
you cannot just thoughtlessly cut down trees,
regardless of whether they have been planted
or grown naturally." After all these years, that
experience and my father's words remain
etched in my memory.

山 SAN 川 SEN 草 SŌ 木 MOKU

These four words, meaning *mountains, rivers, grass* and *trees,* can be combined in Japanese to form a single compound word, which then expresses the idea of *nature* or *scenery.*

早春雨上り　After the rain

待ちわびた春　Long awaited blooming

山里の紅梅　Mountain plum blossoms

春夕　Spring evening

谷の山桜　Blossoms above the gorge

高原初夏　Early summer in the highlands

暁光笠ヶ岳　Early morning light——Mt. Kasagatake | 35

夏草茂る　Leafy curtain

ヒトツバ群落　Green clusters of *Hitotsuba*

豪雨の後　Mountain torrent

夕立去る　Free-floating forms

湿原の風　Windblown marsh

48 溪谷晚夏 Late summer gorge

初秋の山なみ　Early autumn landscape

滝遥か　Distant waterfall

秋霖　Rain-drenched forest floor

晩秋八甲田　Hakkoda in late autumn

秋の吾妻渓谷 Agatsuma Valley tints

霧氷の川辺　Silver thaw along the river

草叢の一葉　Vagrant leaf

斜光に映える　Trees glanced by sunlight

穂高雪嶺　Mt. Hotaka's snowy parapet

八ヶ岳旭光　*Morning light behind Mt. Yatsugatake*

PHOTOGRAPHIC DATA

13——LINHOF SUPER TECHNIKA 4x5 TELE-XENAR 360mm F5.5 f22 1/8
14——HASSELBLAD 500C/M TELE-TESSAR 500mm F8 f16 1/8
15——HASSELBLAD 500C/M SONNAR 250mm F5.6 f22 1/15
16——HASSELBLAD SWC BIOGON 38mm F4.5 f16 1/8
17——HASSELBLAD 500C/M SONNAR 150mm F4 f22 1/4
18——HASSELBLAD 500C/M TELE-TESSAR 500mm F8 f22 1/8
19——HASSELBLAD 500C/M SONNAR 150mm F4 f22 1/15
20——HASSELBLAD 500C/M DISTAGON 60mm F3.5 f22 1/15
21——HASSELBLAD 500C/M TELE-TESSAR 500mm F8 f32 1/4
22——HASSELBLAD 500C/M DISTAGON 60mm F3.5 f11 1/60
23——HASSELBLAD 500C/M TELE-TESSAR 500mm F8 f32 1/8
24——HASSELBLAD SWC BIOGON 38mm F4.5 f8 1/8
25——HASSELBLAD 500C/M SONNAR 250mm F5.6 f22 1/8
26——LINHOF SUPER TECHNIKA 4x5 FUJINON 400mm F8 f32 1/8
27——LINHOF SUPER TECHNIKA 4x5 NIKKOR 210mm F5.6 f32 1/4
28·29——TOYO FIELD 8x10 FUJINON 300mm F5.6 f32 1/4
30——LINHOF SUPER TECHNIKA 4x5 TELE-XENAR 360mm F5.5 f22 1/4
31——LINHOF SUPER TECHNIKA 4x5 TELE-XENAR 360mm F5.5 f32 1/4
32——HASSELBLAD SWC BIOGON 38mm F4.5 f22 1/8
33——HASSELBLAD 500C/M TELE-TESSAR 500mm F8 f22 1/8
34——HASSELBLAD 500C/M TELE-TESSAR 500mm F8 f32 1/8
35——HASSELBLAD 500C/M PLANAR 100mm F3.5 f22 1/8
36——HASSELBLAD SWC BIOGON 38mm F4.5 f11 1/30
37——HASSELBLAD SWC BIOGON 38mm F4.5 f16 1/8
38——LINHOF SUPER TECHNIKA 4x5 FUJINON 400mm F8 f32 1/8
39——LINHOF SUPER TECHNIKA 4x5 FUJINON 250mm F6.3 f32 1/4
40——HASSELBLAD SWC BIOGON 38mm F4.5 f22 1sec.
41——LINHOF SUPER TECHNIKA 4x5 FUJINON 400mm F8 f32 1/2
42——HASSELBLAD 500C/M TELE-TESSAR 500mm F8 f22 1/15
43——HASSELBLAD 500C/M DISTAGON 60mm F3.5 f11 1/60
44——HASSELBLAD 500C/M TELE-TESSAR 500mm F8 f22 1/15
45——HASSELBLAD SWC BIOGON 38mm F4.5 f16 1/8
46——HASSELBLAD 500C/M SONNAR 250mm F5.6 f32 1sec.
47——HASSELBLAD 500C/M DISTAGON 60mm F3.5 f22 1/15
48——HASSELBLAD 500C/M SONNAR 250mm F5.6 f22 1/8
49——HASSELBLAD SWC BIOGON 38mm F4.5 f22 1sec.
50——LINHOF SUPER TECHNIKA 4x5 NIKKOR 150mm F5.6 f32 1/8
51——LINHOF SUPER TECHNIKA 4x5 NIKKOR 210mm F5.6 f16 1/30
52——HASSELBLAD 500C/M TELE-TESSAR 500mm F8 f45 1/4
53——HASSELBLAD 500C/M SONNAR 250mm F5.6 f32 1/8
54——LINHOF SUPER TECHNIKA 4x5 FUJINON 400mm F8 f22 1/8
55——LINHOF SUPER TECHNIKA 4x5 TELE-XENAR 360mm F5.5 f32 1/8
56——HASSELBLAD 500C/M SONNAR 250mm F5.6 f16 1/15

57——LINHOF SUPER TECHNIKA 4x5 TELE-XENAR 360mm F5.5 f32 1/8 (F)
58——HASSELBLAD 500C/M DISTAGON 60mm F3.5 f16 1/30
59——HASSELBLAD 500C/M SONNAR 250mm F5.6 f22 1/8
60——HASSELBLAD 500C/M SONNAR 250mm F5.6 f22 1/2
61——HASSELBLAD 500C/M SONNAR 250mm F5.6 f32 1/4
62——HASSELBLAD 500C/M SONNAR 150mm F4 f22 1/8 (F)
63——HASSELBLAD 500C/M SONNAR 250mm F5.6 f22 1/8
64——LINHOF SUPER TECHNIKA 4x5 FUJINON 400mm F8 f16 2sec.
65——TOYO FIELD 4x5 FUJINON 600mm F11 f16 1sec. (F)
66——HASSELBLAD 500C/M SONNAR 250mm F5.6 f22 1/8
67——HASSELBLAD 500C/M SONNAR 150mm F4 f32 1/4
68·69——TOYO FIELD 8x10 FUJINON 600mm F11 f45 1/2
70——LINHOF SUPER TECHNIKA 4x5 FUJINON 400mm F8 f32 1/8
71——HASSELBLAD 500C/M DISTAGON 60mm F3.5 f22 1/8
72——HASSELBLAD 500C/M SONNAR 250mm F5.6 f32 1/8
73——HASSELBLAD 500C/M SONNAR 250mm F5.6 f32 1/8
74——HASSELBLAD 500C/M SONNAR 250mm F5.6 f22 1/8 (F)
75——HASSELBLAD SWC BIOGON 38mm F4.5 f22 1/8
76——LINHOF SUPER TECHNIKA 4x5 FUJINON 400mm F8 f22 1/4
77——LINHOF SUPER TECHNIKA 4x5 FUJINON 400mm F8 f32 1/4
78——HASSELBLAD 500C/M SONNAR 250mm F5.6 f32 1/8
79——HASSELBLAD 500C/M TELE-TESSAR 500mm F8 f32 1/4
80——HASSELBLAD 500C/M SONNAR 150mm F4 f32 1/8
81——HASSELBLAD 500C/M SONNAR 250mm F5.6 f32 1/4
82——HASSELBLAD 500C/M PLANAR 100mm F3.5 f16 1/8
83——HASSELBLAD 500C/M DISTAGON 38mm F4.5 f22 1/4
84——LINHOF SUPER TECHNIKA 4x5 FUJINON 400mm F8 f32 1/4
85——LINHOF SUPER TECHNIKA 4x5 NIKKOR 150mm F5.6 f16 1/8 (F)
86——HASSELBLAD 500C/M SONNAR 250mm F5.6 f22 1/8
87——LINHOF SUPER TECHNIKA 4x5 FUJINON 400mm F8 f22 1/8
88——LINHOF SUPER TECHNIKA 4x5 FUJINON 400mm F8 f32 1/15
89——HASSELBLAD 500C/M SONNAR 250mm F5.6 f22 1/60
90——LINHOF SUPER TECHNIKA 4x5 FUJINON 400mm F8 f32 1/30
91——HASSELBLAD 500C/M SONNAR 250mm F5.6 f16 1/250
92——HASSELBLAD 500C/M SONNAR 150mm F4 f22 1/8
93——HASSELBLAD 500C/M PLANAR 100mm F3.5 f11 1/8
94——HASSELBLAD 500C/M PLANAR 100mm F3.5 f16 1/8
95——LINHOF SUPER TECHNIKA 4x5 FUJINON 400mm F8 f22 1/15
96——LINHOF SUPER TECHNIKA 4x5 FUJINON 400mm F8 f16 1sec.

FILM——表示のないものは，EKTACHROME (EPR ASA 64) を使用。
　　　　　FUJICHROME (RFP ASA 50) を使用したものは、(F) と表示。

あとがき
前田真三

この『山川草木』と題する写真集は、数年前「日本の自然」シリーズの第一巻として出版した『一木一草』の姉妹編ともいえるものである。このシリーズではその後『上高地』、『奥三河』、『丘の四季』と特定の地域に限定されたものが続いたので、今回は一般的な日本の風景を「山川草木」と題して編集したものである。とりたてて特色という程の事でもないが、巻頭にモノクロームの頁をつくったことと、本文中では季節に分類することをせず、全体的には遠景を少なく中景から近景のものを比較的多くして、日本の風景の持つ繊細な美しさと力強さを表現するよう心がけて編集した。

さてグラフィック社刊のこのシリーズは本書を含めて五巻となり、既刊のものは好評裡に版を重ねている。その今日に至るまでの経過を簡単にふり返ってみたいと思う。

私は十年前に写業十周年を記念して『出合の瞬間』という写真集を出版した。この写真集で私はいくつかの新しい試みをしてみた。まず従来の風景写真と全く違った題名を選定した事である。私はかねがね「風景は出合った瞬間が一番美しい」という持論を持っていたので、それをそのままストレートに題名とした。判形は横型を選んだ。従来の写真集は圧倒的に縦型が多かったが、風景写真は横位置の写真が多く、横型の方がより効果的であると考えたからである。また編集方法も、余り四季にこだわることなく、見開きの左右の写真がそれぞれ相乗効果を上げる様な組み合わせを重視した。そして日本の風景の持つ落ち着いた色調を再現する為、マット調の紙を採用した。その他国際情勢も考え、簡単な英文を付記したり、様々な工夫をこらしたが、結果は価格が高すぎたこと、少々凝りすぎたことなどいくつかの反省点もあり、広く一般の話題になるほどではなかった。ただ非常に高く評価してくれた人も多く、私自身将来に向けてひとつ

の結論を得たという点でも成功であったと思う。

そして五年間が経過した。今度は十五周年を記念し、『出合の瞬間』を原形に、いくつかの点を改善して、『一木一草』という写真集の編集にとりかかった。当初自費出版のつもりであったが、折も折グラフィック社から写真集の話が持ち上り、これを共同製作の形で上梓することになった。ここでは協力して徹底的にコストダウンを計り、また国際性も重視してすべて英文併記にすることにした。時代背景も手伝ってか、この『一木一草』は予想外の反響を呼んだ。そして海外を含め従来の自然写真の購読者とは違った全く新しい多くの需要層を開拓することができた。

十年前は横型の判形は書店の書架からとび出すので嫌われる等という理由で、ほとんどの出版社が採用していなかったが、今では書店に横型の写真集が氾濫していることを思うと一人感慨深いものがある。

風景写真を撮り始めて今年で丁度二十年になる。風景写真を撮ることはある意味では純然たる肉体労働である。従って、体力だけで写真を撮っていると、歳をとるにつれて、知らず知らずのうちに写真の質も低下する恐れがある。しかし、歳を重ねることによって写真技術や人生経験を積むわけであるから、それらを総合的にうまく生かすことによって、体力の低下を十分カバーできる筈である。また良い作品を創る為には、それなりの環境作りも大切な要素であると思う。そういった意味も含めて私は昨年北海道美瑛町に拓真館という前進基地を建設した。ここしばらくは、この地での写真活動が中心になると思うが、更に深く自然と密着した生活の中から、密度の濃い、そして質の高い写真作りに専念したいと考えている昨今である。

AFTERWORD
Shinzo Maeda

"This Land......This Beauty——Japan's Natural Splendor" is the latest book in the "Natural Beauty of Japan" series which I began several years ago with "A Tree, A Blade of Grass." Three later volumes in the series, "Kamikochi——The Nippon Alps," "Okumik-awa," and "Hills of Color," were the result of work in limited geographical areas, but the scenes in the present volume are drawn from all over Japan. In addition, this time I have added a few pages of monochrome photos at the beginning of the book. "This Land......This Beauty" also differs from the others in that it does not have its main sections arranged by seasons. And I have reduced the number of distant views while increasing middle distance and close-up shots in order to display both the power and the delicate beauty of Japanese scenery.

Since the four volumes which the Graphic-sha Publishing Company has so far produced have been well received and have gone into reprints, it may be appropriate to briefly look back on the history of our efforts so far. In 1977 I published a collection of photos entitled "The Moment of Encounter" to commemorate my ten years in photography. In that work, I adopted several new approaches. First of all, I chose a title which was quite different from the type usually found on scenic photography books. I have always held the notion that scenery is most beautiful at the very moment we come across it, and this idea was behind the book's brief, "direct" title.
The format of the book was another departure from conventional photography publishing. Almost all earlier books in the genre were vertical rectangles because bookstores did not like the way long books stuck out from their shelves. But I realized that since most shots of scenery were horizontal, that format would be more appropriate in a book of such photos. In editing the book, I paid little attention to arranging the photographs by seasons; I was more concerned with the balance and co-ordination of pairs of pictures on adjacent pages, and with the soft tones of Japanese scenery, which I tried to capture through the use of mat-type papers. Finally, with possible international sales in mind, simple English translations were added. It may be that I had a surplus of ideas, for the book was overly elaborate and production costs made it too expensive; sales were disappointing. Nevertheless, I found that many people rated the book highly, and in one sense it was a success because the experience I gained pointed out directions for my later work.
Five years after the publication of "The Moment of Encounter," I decided to mark my fifteenth year of work with the volume of photos entitled "A Tree, A Blade of Grass," an outgrowth of "The Moment of Encounter" which embodied more new ideas. Originally I planned to publish it myself, but fortunately I had the opportunity to co-publish with Graphic-sha, and this time we tried to cut costs as much as possible, though we did decide to have a text with both Japanese and an English translation. The book had an unexpected reception; we found that both in Japan and overseas, it attracted many new kinds of purchasers who were quite different from those who usually buy nature photography books.

Almost two decades have passed since I first started taking scenic photographs. The task involved in such photography is, in a way, pure physical work. There-fore, if I use only my physical energy in producing pictures, age may cause the quality of my work to diminish year by year without my noticing it. However, the older I get, the more I gain in experience and photographic technique, and I feel that if I carefully approach my work in a total way, I can hope to completely compensate for the loss of my physical strength and energy.
I also believe that good work requires a good environment. Partly for that reason, last year I built a "base studio" called Takushinkan in Biei Town on Hokkaido, and for some time in the future, I will be mainly operating out of and around that location. I hope it will provide closer contacts with nature and enable me to work in a way that will enrich the quality of my photography.

1922 ● 東京都八王子市下恩方町に生まれる
Born in Shimo-Ongata-cho, Hachioji City, Tokyo

1948 ● ニチメン㈱に入社、以後17年間勤務
Employed by Nichimen Corporation, works there for the next 17 years

1967 ● フォト・エージェンシー㈱丹渓を設立、代表となり、同時に写真活動に入る
Founds Tankei Photo Agency Co., Ltd., becomes it's representative and a professional photographer

1974 ● 写真集「ふるさとの四季」(毎日新聞社)
Publishes "The Four Seasons of a Home Town" (The Mainichi Newspapers)

1976 ● 写真集「日本の彩」(旅行読売出版社)
写真集「ふるさとの山河」(毎日新聞社)
Publishes "The Colors of Japan" (Ryoko Yomiuri Publishing Co.)
Publishes "Mountains and Rivers of a Home Town" (The Mainichi Newspapers)

1977 ● 写真集「出合の瞬間」(毎日新聞社)
Publishes "The Moment of Encounter" (The Mainichi Newspapers)

1978 ● 写真集「春夏秋冬」(国際情報社)
Publishes "Spring, Summer, Autumn and Winter" (Kokusai Johosha Publishing Co.)

1981 ● 写真集「北海道——大地の詩」(集英社)
Publishes "Hokkaido—Poetry of the Earth" (Shueisha Publishing Co.)

1982 ● 写真集「山河有情」(保育社)
Publishes "Scenes from Nature" (Hoikusha Publishing Co.)

1983 ● 写真集「一木一草」(グラフィック社)
写真集「昭和写真全仕事・前田真三」(朝日新聞社)
Publishes "A Tree, A Blade of Grass" (Graphic-sha Publishing Co.)
Publishes "Shinzo Maeda" (Asahi Shimbun Publishing Campany)

1984 ● 写真集「上高地」(グラフィック社)
写真集「ランドスケープ・フォトグラフィー」(共著 アメリカ・アムフォト)
日本写真協会年度賞を受賞
Publishes "The Nippon Alps, Kamikochi" (Graphic-sha Publishing Co.)
Participates the book, "Landscape Photography" (Amphoto, U.S.A.)
Receives the Annual Award for the Photographic Society of Japan

1985 ● 写真集「奥三河」(グラフィック社)
写真集「四季百景」(日本カメラ社)
写真集「山野逍通」(毎日新聞社)
第39回毎日出版文化賞特別賞を受賞(「奥三河」)
Publishes "Okumikawa" (Graphic-sha Publishing Co.)
Publishes "Scenes in Four Seasons" (Nippon Camera Publishing Co.)
Publishes "Ambling in Nature" (The Mainichi Newspapers)
Receives Special Award at the Thirty-ninth Mainichi Publications Culture Competition for the book "Okumikawa"

1986 ● 写真集「丘の四季」(グラフィック社)
北海道美瑛町に自然スタジオ拓真館を建設
Publishes "Hills of Color—Scenes and Seasons" (Graphic-sha Publishing Co.)
Establishes nature studio 'Takushinkan' in Biei-cho, Hokkaido

1987 ● 写真集「白い幻想」(講談社)
Publishes "White Fantasy" (Kodansha Ltd.)

office ● 前田真三写真事務所　株式会社 丹渓 〒107 東京都港区北青山2-7-26 メゾン青山402 TEL(03)405-1681
TANKEI CO., LTD. 402 MAISON AOYAMA 2-7-26 KITA-AOYAMA MINATO-KU TOKYO 〒107 PHONE (03)405-1681

山川草木　撮影 前田真三
THIS LAND··· THIS BEAUTY
Japan's Natural Splendor
1987年 6月25日　初版第一刷発行

定価 ● 3,800円　乱丁・落丁はお取替えいたします。

発 行 者 ● 久世利郎
発 行 所 ● 株式会社グラフィック社
　　　　　〒102 東京都千代田区九段北1-19-12　PHONE 03-263-4318
製作協力 ● フォトライブラリー㈱丹渓
印　　刷 ● 凸版印刷株式会社
製　　本 ● 凸版印刷株式会社
写　　植 ● 三和写真工芸株式会社